FIRST STEPS
a mentored guide to start rebuilding your purity

mentor manual series: module one

First Steps: A Mentored Guide to Start Rebuilding Your Purity
Mentor Manual Series: Module One

Published by Pure Life Alliance
www.purelifealliance.org
info@purelifealliance.org

ISBN-13: 978-1523821792
ISBN-10: 1523821795

Cover & inside graphics: dreamstime.com
Cover design: Blake Williams
Design layout: Blake Williams, CJ Chang

DEDICATION

To all the men who have walked this journey before you.
They are proof that it is possible and that you can do it.

CONTENTS

FOREWORD

The road of **recovery** has always been one that is unpredictable, yet exciting; fearful, yet hopeful; disappointing, yet encouraging; and challenging, yet progressing. In actuality, everyone is on a recovery journey. All have fallen short of God's glory—and in our human depravity all are drawn to that which indulges the flesh with gratification. Throughout Scriptures we see how man is in desperate need of God's help to overcome the deadly results of sin and the wicked heart—and how He sent Jesus to do what we could not do on our own. In brokenness we come to the place where we acknowledge our utter dependence upon God. And with compassion Jesus becomes our ultimate Mentor—the One who has the experience and wisdom to guide us toward healing and victory.

God provides a number of ways to assist us on the healing journey. He has given us His Son Jesus as a model; His Word as a lamp for our feet to stay on the path; prayer as means to go directly to Him with all of our needs, concerns and thanksgiving; the Holy Spirit to guide, convict and empower as He lives within us; other people to encourage, correct, teach, rebuke and pray for us. This manual focuses to a great extent upon the gift of having someone who has walked ahead in the journey to assist us in our adventure. We call that being mentored!

The accomplished NFL football coach Tony Dungy, in his book *The Mentor Leader: Secrets to Building People and Teams That Win Consistently*, said: "Remember that mentor leadership is all about serving. Jesus said, 'For even the Son of Man came not to be served but to serve others and to give his life as a ransom for many (Mark 10:45).' "

What a thrill to be able to guide another on the journey that we ourselves have been traveling—sort of sounds like discipleship, doesn't it? One of the signs of maturity is the ability to recognize that life is not lived well alone. A mentor is a guide who joins us so that we don't walk alone. Being mentored requires humility and the willingness to be open to the power of the relationship with the mentor, for "as iron sharpens iron, so one person sharpens another" (Prov. 27:17).

Friends, this is the picture of community. God provides community to assist us in becoming more like Him. One person put it this way: "A community of grace gently insists that we are lovingly honest with each other and ourselves about our sin and our needs. In openness and vulnerability, we can lay it all out on the table, and in return, receive a depth of love and protection that we never imagined. This, in turn, leads to the freedom to be transformed and truly move into maturity" (Holly C., *Bo's Café* Amazon.com review).

May God richly bless all who lovingly mentor and all who courageously follow!

—Dennis Henderson, Psy.D. (George Fox University)
Licensed Psychologist
Vice-President of Provider Relations
Western Psychological and Counseling Services

KEY

In the hopes that this manual becomes a lasting resource, we have included some helpful indicators in each of the lessons.

QR Codes

Several QR codes are included to allow you to view short relevant videos. If you do not have one already, consider downloading a QR code app on your smartphone so you can enhance your learning process. URLs are also provided if you would prefer to view them on your computer.

https://goo.gl/Dt8Ny5

Assignments

You will find assignments purposefully scattered throughout the manual. You may be tempted to skip the assignments, or at least make a halfhearted attempt to complete them. No one will be grading your assignments—this is not a classroom, it is real life—but know that you will only get out of this manual what you put into it. Determine now to take the time and invest the effort the assignments require. We know you will be glad you did.

▨▨▨ ASSIGNMENT ▨▨▨

Discuss With Your Mentor

The best resource God offers you through this manual is your **mentor**. He will share much of himself with you over the coming weeks. Trust him. He is further down the road than you are and has great insight into the journey. The apostle Paul said, "Join in imitating me, brothers, and observe those who live according to the example you have in us" (Philippians 3:17). Keep this in mind as you talk with your mentor!

INTRODUCTION
Welcome to the Journey

There is a lot included in the phrase "Welcome to the Journey." As you study the eight lessons included in *First Steps: A Mentored Guide to Start Rebuilding Your Purity, Module One*, you will begin to get a sense of the path that lies before you. For now, consider four key ideas that will help craft your understanding of your next steps.

1. You were not in the club, but now you are.

Chances are—if you are like many men—you have lost count of how many times you longed to stop your out-of-control behavior. "When am I going to stop doing this? I just can't seem to break free of this." It was a desperate expression of this question for a final time that has prompted you to get help.

A key reason you have not been able to claim victory over this sexual area is because you have kept it hidden. You have literally been alone. You have chosen to be alone. But now you have made a different choice. This time, you have decided to get real help. Paul says God "will bring to light what is hidden in darkness and reveal the intentions of the hearts" (1 Corinthians 4:5, HCSB).

God has handed you a club membership card. You do not have to struggle alone anymore.

2. It is not an exclusive club.

Years ago, American Express used the slogan "Membership has its privileges." For all intents and purposes, it was a rich person's credit card. If you were a card-carrying member of American Express, it said something about you. You had made it. And a limitless credit card was one of your rewards.

For Men Only (**FMO**) group membership is not like an American Express membership. The group you have joined is for men who need help. That means you! It is for men of all backgrounds, faiths and ages—and yes, even degrees of sexual sin. It is an everyman's club membership, open for all.

But do not misunderstand. FMO group membership does have its privileges—the key one being open, honest, real community that empowers your choices to live pure in an impure world.

3. It is a long road, not quickly accomplished.

You have been welcomed to a journey. This journey has a definitive start, but no finish line—not here on Earth, at least. During the next few months, you will begin to understand the importance of getting rid of what we call "**destination thinking**."

Destination thinking says:

- "I'll get to where I won't have to struggle with **purity** anymore." This is a lie.

- "If I can't get to the end of this struggle, I'm not as good as other men who have." This is a lie.

- "If I work really hard on this for the next few weeks or months, I can finally beat this and I'll be free from that point on." This is mostly a lie.

Our best counsel for you is to settle in and stay engaged. You should expect to be in your group anywhere from 3 to 5 years. Do not believe the lies that tell you real healing is a quick process. It is not. Real healing goes much deeper than just stopping unhealthy sexual behavior. The truths you will learn in your FMO group eventually apply to every area of your life. And this takes time; there are no shortcuts.

4. It is characterized by camaraderie.

One of the best advantages of joining an FMO group is the help you will gain from other men on the journey. Do not picture yourself all alone out in the desert, desperate for water or food, with no help in sight. View your next steps as one of a group of guys traveling together. When one gets held up—figuratively—by a stone in his shoe, everyone stops with him and waits. If another man trips and falls flat on his face, when he lifts his head and looks around he will see his group coming back to help him stand up again. When—not if—you screw up and sin sexually, your group will be there to support your choices and help you discover better ways to live in purity.

Camaraderie is characterized by an engaged mindset. Trust is not built without a sense of safety and mutual concern. The journey you are taking now must include an element of safe risk. That is to say, we believe the best group meeting means you have shared almost too vulnerably. "Maybe I shouldn't have shared what I did just now. I don't know if I can trust these guys." The courage to share vulnerably is what creates a robust relationship among men.

There is a first truth to hold onto: your group is safe. And because it is safe, you can share things about yourself that no one knows. When you risk this, you have contributed to the intensity of your group's bond and increased the measure of trust and **authenticity** that they have offered you.

There is great purity just up ahead. You—and the men God has placed in your life, your FMO group—will be moving toward a freedom known only by men who share a dissatisfaction with their sexual sin.

Welcome to the Journey!

LESSON ONE
It's a Journey, Not a Destination

One of the first concepts you will need to grasp is that this is "a journey, not a destination." This is likely the last idea you want to hear at this point. You want a quick, easy solution to solve the problems you are facing. But the healing journey out of habitual sexual sin is a multi-year journey. It takes a long time to gain lasting victory over past enslavement to **lust**. There are a number of reasons for this, but it is enough right now to hear that this is not a quick, easy formula.

Journey thinking allows for time to heal. It provides process time to heal, not just on the outside (behaviors), but in a lasting way on the inside (longings, belief system) as well.

There are many people who teach that purity is primarily about stopping behavior. They use words like "Just stop it," or "If you just read your Bible and pray more, God will deliver you from these sins." Unfortunately, the message this communicates is an emphasis on **behaviorism**. It also proves to be impossible and leaves us feeling worse than before. Repeated failure convinces us that we will never change. It moves us to believe we are worse than those around us. If we were better, we would be able to "stop it."

https://goo.gl/uZYDfm

For a lighthearted view of this behavioral focus, scan the adjacent QR code. It will take you to a humorous skit about a psychologist, portrayed by Bob Newhart. A woman comes into his office with a strange fear. As he "helps" her "overcome" her fear, notice how futile his counsel is and how disillusioned his client becomes.

"Stop it!" has a quick focus. It is designed to get results fast—with as little engagement from others as possible. It disregards the nature of real change. Helping someone with real change means an investment in relationship and the process of investing in someone's life over the long haul.

In the devotional book *Dare to Journey with Henri Nouwen*, Charles Ringma writes:

> Nouwen reminds us that care means to be present to the other person and warns that "cure without care makes us preoccupied with quick changes, impatient and unwilling to share each other's burden."

> This warning is well placed. We are usually quick in offering our counseling, healing, and helping strategies, and tend to blame the other for a lack of commitment to our strategies if results are not forthcoming. We find it much more difficult to journey with others, enter their places of pain as they are opened to us, offer friendship even when there is no significant change, and seek to empower rather than help.[1]

A man or woman focused on a healthy journey toward purity should expect to spend three to five years working toward freedom. Three to five years! That is a lot longer than most of us are willing to engage. Some

---

[1] Ringma, Charles. *Dare to Journey with Henri Nouwen*. NavPress, 2000.

believe they can rush the process. But the truth is this process will not be rushed. It cannot be rushed because it involves much more than just stopping habitual sexual sin. The healthy journey involves significant heart change. If you are a Christian, it involves a re-crafting of your understanding of the Gospel. A healthy journey ultimately lasts for the rest of your life.

Here are a couple questions for you to consider:

- How long have you been struggling with sexual sin?
- How long is reasonable to think it might take you to finally break free?

Let's break it down into actual years. If you are 35 years old, you have probably struggled with sexual sin for the last 20 years of your life. To be generous, it is likely closer to 25 years, but either number is a huge part of your life. So for 2/3 of your life, lust has reigned. How long should we expect the healing journey to be? Is six months long enough? How about two years? Remember, you have behavior patterns, beliefs and inner longings you have been fueling for most of your life.

Let's say you are working hard at breaking free from this feeling of enslavement to lust. You join an FMO group. You even start seeing a counselor. You regularly do your reading assignments for group and attend every week. And after a few months, you and your wife (if you are married) spend 30 minutes each week talking about your healing. Altogether, over the course of a year you will likely spend less than 250 hours working on your recovery. By comparison, if you viewed magazines or online pornography for just four hours a week, that was also 250 hours, but that was per year. For 20 years that is 5,000 hours indulging in lust. How can 250 hours of work break the habits a person spent 5,000 hours creating?

So let's think again. How long should we expect the healing journey to be? We would counsel you to keep your eyes on a five-year journey. If God brings you through faster than that, great! If not, stay engaged and keep on the journey.

Destination thinking misleads you by saying, "I want to be done with this. I will get past this and not have to worry about it. I will finally arrive at being pure (the destination)." Yet you are just beginning a journey. It is a long and difficult one with lots of joys and many pains. When you believe you are on a journey, you will have the stamina to keep pressing on. When you fall down—and you will—destination thinking can take you out. Journey thinking, on the other hand, sees that slip in light of the long process of crafting purity in you.

Remember: it's a journey, not a destination.

ASSIGNMENT

WRITING YOUR STORY

Telling stories is one of the longest traditions in all of human history. A story told well is meant to communicate important truths. Sharing stories can be a powerful experience of change for those hearing it, as well as the one sharing it.

Writing your story is a first step of vulnerably sharing yourself with others. As one who has wrestled with unhealthy sexual behavior, you have regularly relied on not telling your story. When we are caught in our sexual sin we want nothing to do with being known for who we think we are. That mindset must end as we begin writing a thoughtful, truthful account of our sexual history.

There are a few things to keep in mind as you tackle this first assignment:

Write a little bit at a time

Writing your story has potential for bringing great healing but it requires you to relive many painful and **triggering** experiences. This is an important aspect of healing, but has the possibility of causing you to feel badly about yourself. When done all at once, the concentration of trauma and your behavior can be overwhelming. Spend 10 to 15 minutes a day for the next few days working on your story. Thinking about these things in little bites will keep the **shame** and **guilt** more manageable.

Be honest

Those of us who struggle with defeating sexual sin have lived in lies for too long. This is your opportunity to come clean. Be truthful about who you are and what you've done. You've joined a group of men committed to being honest with you. Step up to the challenge and choose honesty as you write your story.

This is not yet another place for image management. Each of the men in your group have honed that dangerous skill to a fine art. But now they're offering you a place to be truly known. A place to be known, accepted and loved. Honor them and this next part of your journey by choosing to tell a completely honest story about yourself.

Keep it somewhere safe

When we write our stories with enough accuracy to be as healthy as possible, they will feel dangerous. That is because they are! You are recording vulnerable things about yourself. This information must not be seen by someone who is not safe. Both during and after writing your story, be extremely cautious about where you keep it. Consider your written story at least as important as your wallet or car keys. Keep it somewhere safe.

Stay in regular communication with your mentor

You will remember reading in the introduction that you are now no longer alone. Practically speaking, what that means for writing your story is that your mentor is never far away. If you are struggling to describe part of your journey, give him a call. If you are being triggered and tempted to sin sexually as you think through past behavior, text him and ask for prayer. Since writing your story can be a tough challenge, consider your mentor a God-given resource for these exact situations.

Consider these questions as you begin to write your story

- When you were growing up, what was your family like?

- How many siblings? Did you live near extended family? Are you from a blended family? What kind of relationships did you have with your dad, mom, brothers and sisters?

• How were you treated? How did you treat others?

• Describe both the behaviors that were done to you (good and bad) as well as the feelings that went with them. Be sure to also write about your treatment of other family members and friends.

• How did you feel about yourself?

• Feelings are difficult for us at this stage of the healing journey. Try to expand the number of words in your vocabulary that talk about emotion. Remember, no emotion is wrong. So be brave and think through your feelings.

• When was your first sexual exposure? Were there others involved?

• What was your experience with self-stimulation and masturbation?

• What did your sexual behavior include? Frequency? How long have these habits been a part of your life?

• When and how did **disclosure** occur? The key distinction here is whether you came forward on your own, or were discovered. How were things "found out"?

LESSON TWO

Facing the Past, Finding Hope for the Future

Exploring Your Story

During your last lesson, you were given an assignment to write your own story. Read this to your mentor now.

Questions to discuss with your mentor:

- In what ways did you try to cover up your behavior?

- In what ways did you deny to yourself that this was a problem, or that it was not hurting yourself or others?

- How has your behavior hurt yourself – your self-esteem, your job, your health, your finances?

- How has your behavior hurt your relationship with God?

- How has your behavior hurt your friendships with other men?

- How has your behavior hurt your relationships with women? Girlfriends?

- How has your behavior hurt your parents?

- If you have children, how has your behavior hurt them?

- How has your behavior hurt your relationship(s) with your wife?

You may think that you are unusual, or that this kind of behavior is rare, especially among men who claim to be Christian. You are not the most despicable man on earth, even though you might feel that way now. Many of us have gone through similar experiences.

Let's discuss some things we have found that don't work:

Keeping it secret does not work—in fact, being honest and exposing everything to a small, safe group will be the greatest step to breaking its power.

Trying harder does not work either, because, believe it or not, none of us have the willpower to overcome these drives and the way we have programmed our brain to behave.

Hoping that it will go away after a passage of time does not work, either —it only gets worse.

What we must realize is that we are completely powerless to stop this behavior on our own.

ASSIGNMENT

LISTING CONSEQUENCES

Take a 3x5 index card or create a note on your phone. Write several things that could happen to your life—things you could lose—if you do not change your behavior. We call these consequences if we do not change.

━━━ ASSIGNMENT ━━━

WRITE AN ACCOUNTABILITY LINE

In order to get started on our road to recovery, we have all had to admit that we could not do it by ourselves. We start with being accountable to a small group, and getting phone numbers to call when we are facing temptation. Initially we create an **Accountability Line**. This is a list of just a few of the most hurtful behaviors that we feel we must stop right now.

So, take the index card you used above or go to the note on your phone, and create a list of two or three behaviors you want to stop today. Label this list "Away from Impurity." When you meet with your mentor and others in your recovery group, you will check in and share honestly about whether you did any of those things in the last week. Avoid the temptation to make a long list. There are always more things to work on, but none of us have enough willpower to work on them all at once. We only find success in working on small numbers of behaviors at a time. Just start with the most destructive ones for now.

> *Accountability Line*
>
> Away From Impurity:
> · no strip clubs
> · no pornography
> Needs:
> · to be valued
> · to make a difference
> Toward Purity:
> · call a man each day
> · reading homework

This early in your recovery, you may not understand the emotional issues that drive you toward your sexual behavior, but over time you will address these. Write the label "Needs." List any emotions that you think may drive you toward sexual acting out. For example, many of us are driven to sexual behaviors when we feel like a failure, not good enough, inadequate, insecure, alone or abandoned—or when we are reminded of childhood shame or abuse.

As part three of your Accountability Line, create a short list of actions you will begin taking "Toward Purity" now in order to heal your brokenness; things like regular attendance at your group, being accountable to the group, calling your mentor, and doing your reading and homework.

This will serve as a good start for you to measure your growth. Each week you will share your successes and failures in moving away from impurity and toward purity with your mentor and **support group**. Throughout your journey you will update this accountability line with the help of your mentor and support group as you learn more about yourself and as you grow past this initial starting point.

One important note about moving toward purity: although men typically do not like talking about their feelings, we have found that it is critical for all of us to do. It is essential to stay in contact with your mentor and other members of your group. Make it a high priority. The main thing to communicate at this point is how you are feeling. The reasons behind this will become clearer over time, but for now we simply want you to begin learning that we run to lust to escape negative emotions, not because of our sex drive.

Counseling

Many of us have found it very helpful to meet with a credible Christian counselor. There are often a number of issues that are beneath our sexual behavior that go beyond what a group has time or expertise to deal with. We highly encourage every man to spend some time with a qualified counselor to unpack these issues.

You can find a Christian counselor in our annual counselor directory or at www.purelifealliance.org/counselors.

ASSIGNMENT

LETTER TO MYSELF

Write a short letter, addressed to yourself, explaining why you do not want to continue in a life driven by lust. Keep this with your Accountability Line; share this with your mentor. He may also share his with you.

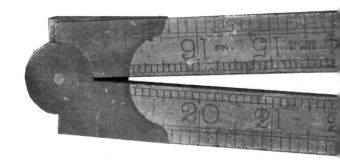

LESSON THREE
Disclosure and Rebuilding Trust

To whom should you disclose past sexual sins and behaviors? Essentially, anyone you hope to have a close relationship with. It is only through deeper connection with other people that you will ever find lasting joy. To be accepted for who you are is essential, but this can only be done if you are fully known.

> What keeps us out of connection is that we feel we are unworthy of connection.[2]
> —Brené Brown

Being fully known requires us to be vulnerable at a level at which we may not feel comfortable. However, becoming vulnerable is required if we are

---

[2] Brown, Brené. (2010, December). Brené Brown: The Power of Vulnerability [Video file.] Retrieved from www.ted.com/talks/brene_brown_on_vulnerability/transcript

to have any hope of attaining purity. It is a risk, but real relationships—unlike **fantasy** relationships—require risk.

In time, you will need to disclose to close friends. While this seems frightening now, we find that being known by our close friends is deeply healing. You will eventually need to talk to your children if they are old enough. And you need to tell your spouse immediately.

> Before Renee and I could move forward and repair the damage inflicted by the past, I knew I had to come clean with her about everything I had done. I couldn't simply get rid of the porn and start living for the Lord without telling her what had happened. She might have seen the change in me, but the secrets of the past would have created an ever-growing chasm between us.[3]
>
> —Clay Crosse

Be sure to share with your mentor any family members or close friends to whom you need to disclose. If you are married, engaged or dating someone, she needs to know as soon as possible.

Telling a spouse every detail of past sexual sin can be damaging, but you should not withhold any information about the exact kinds of sexual sin you have taken part in or experienced. We will summarize disclosure for you here, but be sure to read Appendix A.

ASSIGNMENT

WHAT YOU SHOULD SHARE

With your mentor, review your story you wrote in Lesson One to discuss what needs to be disclosed and what should be avoided.

Things that need to be disclosed:

- any form of pornography use
- masturbation
- types of sexual behavior involving other people

---

[3] Crosse, Clay. *I Surrender All: Rebuilding a Marriage Broken by Pornography.* NavPress, 2005.

- people's names you have been sexual with, if she knows them
- ways you connected with people to arrange sex
- any pregnancies, abortions or children from your sexual behavior
- financial consequences that your wife is unaware of
- contraction of any STDs

Things you may (but do not have to) disclose:

- sexual experiences as a child
- sexual behavior before engagement/marriage.

Things/details to avoid during disclosure:

- specific websites frequented
- times/places where sexual encounters occurred, names of sexual partners your spouse does not know
- details of sexual encounters (what person wore, physical characteristics, what was done together, what was said).

We advise that you write exactly what you will tell your wife. Then have her read the *Dealing with Disclosure* document and set a time to disclose to her.

When you have this disclosure meeting with her, be sure to give her time to respond. Do not defend yourself; just allow her to say what she needs to say.

http://goo.gl/b0NRhf

Feelings After Disclosure

Disclosure, while frightening, can leave a man feeling relieved. The burden he has carried, possibly for most of his life, has been lifted. His secret is out. He may feel that he is finally taking responsibility for his sin. He knows something new is happening in his life, and it can be exciting.

His spouse, on the other hand, usually feels the exact opposite. This is especially true the longer they were married before disclosure happened. To the spouse, she is just learning that her husband has been lying to her, or

http://goo.gl/Zyz3V8

29

hiding things from her at best, in most cases throughout their entire marriage. She just learned that the man she thought she married never existed. She had risked all in opening herself up to marry him, only to find out he had betrayed her, possibly for years. She does not know if she can ever risk trusting him again. She may feel that, in fact, she doesn't even know him.

Look at the opposing feelings that each spouse typically feels after disclosure and discuss these with your mentor.

HIS REALITY	HER REALITY
I'm becoming a man with strong moral principles	I've been morally betrayed
I love her more now than ever before	I've never felt less loved by him
I'm beginning to see how much I value our marriage	I've never realized until now how little our marriage meant to him

—Ted Roberts, Pure Desire, p.273

Be prepared to feel a disconnect with the encouragement you feel and the discouragement she feels. It is unfair of you to expect her to understand why you feel hope at this point. She will need months to get to a place where she can dare to feel much hope. While this will be very painful for both of you, it is necessary if you want to rebuild trust in your marriage.

Rebuilding Trust

It does not really matter if a wife never knew about her husband's secret sexual sin life, or if she knew all along; it is going to be a long time before she believes that her husband has stopped living that secret life. Even if she did know, the man certainly tried to hide as much of his behavior as he could from her. If she did not know, she is just coming to realize how long and how much he has lied to her. Either way, she is shattered. There is no way around the fact that it is going to be a long time before she can take the risk to trust what her husband tells her again, especially as it relates to his sexual behavior when he is alone or away from home.

What makes this difficult for the man is that he sees and feels that he is changing; perhaps in ways he never thought were possible. He is excited and has renewed hope for a life that he is no longer ashamed of. His wife, on the other hand, remains depressed, distant and untrusting of him. He feels frustrated that she cannot see how much he is changing and how, for the first time ever, he really is becoming trustworthy.

Steps Toward Rebuilding Trust

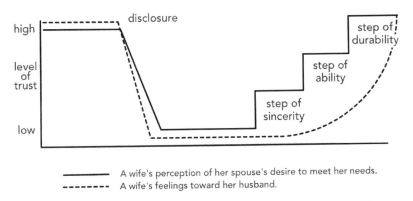

——————— A wife's perception of her spouse's desire to meet her needs.
- - - - - - - A wife's feelings toward her husband.

Friesen, DeLoss D. and Ruby M. *Counseling and Marriage, Vol. 19.* Word Publishing, 1995.

For a wife to trust her husband again, she will need to see evidence over a sustained period of time that he is, in fact, a new man. She will not trust even her own feelings, because her feelings that once told her she could trust him proved to be wrong. The chart above diagrams what has to happen in order for a woman to begin trusting her husband again after learning he has lied for years.

Both lines drop when a wife learns of her husband's behavior (disclosure). She does not perceive him as a safe partner who wants to meet her needs (solid line). Her trust in him is extremely low. Her feelings (dotted line) take much longer to align with her perception of his trustworthiness.

Your wife's feelings are probably lower than you can truly understand. She may not want anything to do with you for a while.

The Step of Sincerity

Next, the man gets serious and begins to participate in an **accountability** group. It is possible his wife will not believe he is actually attending group (depending on how dishonest he has been in the past). But perhaps she sees him doing homework for his group and then has solid evidence that he is at least trying. Here the mismatch between her perception and true feelings begin. He likely feels that since he is trying she should begin to trust him, at least a little. However, she wants to believe that he is going to change, but is still too afraid to trust her own feelings. Your wife's feelings toward you may not improve during this step. This is normal.

The Step of Ability

When he stays engaged in group, a man shows signs that he is not only willing to try, but is actually beginning to change. He begins to pay more attention to what his wife is saying. He spends more time with their children. He watches less TV in order to help the family. He is demonstrating a new ability to connect to his family. He is excited at the changes occurring.

At this point, you may expect your wife's feelings for you to significantly improve. But for a time the distance between her perception and true feelings for you actually get further apart.

A wife may in fact feel threatened by her husband, not understanding why she still does not feel close to him or trust him. To her, this is evidence that her husband does not really understand how much he hurt her in the first place. Out of self-preservation, she typically does not allow herself to believe these changes are permanent. She begins to dare to hope a little that all this is real, but she cannot allow herself to believe it completely.

The Step of Durability

Only when a man stays connected with his **restoration** process and shows evidence that he is engaged with his family over a long period of time does his wife allow herself to begin to trust her husband and have feelings for him again.

How long does all this take? It is different for every couple, but typically it is at least a year before a wife starts trusting her husband again. Until then her feelings might be something like, "I love you, but I don't quite trust you yet." The time varies considerably from couple to couple, and the length of time is not necessarily related to the seriousness of the husband's past sexual actions. **Betrayal** is betrayal, even when the adulterous "sexual partner" is pornography. The number of years a man spent in sexual sin while being married may play a larger role in how long it takes his wife to begin to trust her husband after he begins recovery.

Our wives (and any friends who did not know about our sexual sin) deserve to have time to decide to trust us again. It is important that we be patient with them. Remember, it is our sin, not hers, that caused trust to be broken. Only through consistent improved behavior can we earn trust again. Dr. Doug Weiss states it best when he says your wife should "believe the behavior" that she sees in you.

Questions to discuss with your mentor:

- How can you demonstrate to your wife that you are serious about changing your negative sexual behavior?

- What will you actually do to stop your unwanted behavior?

- How long will you need to keep doing the above in order to show your wife durability in your behavior change?

Your Wife and Accountability

It is common for a wife to try to control her husband's restoration process. This is understandable, given that she wants to do all she can to protect herself from future emotional harm. But if she attempts to monitor her husband and point out his failures, it will be more harmful than helpful.

We do need accountability, and we will set that up within the support group. Part of accountability often includes installing "accountability software" that reports to a couple of men in your group what you are doing

on the Internet.* It is perfectly fine, and likely a good idea, if you add your wife to the list of people who receive your online accountability reports. It is the men in your support group, however, who should be administrating that software, not your wife. Your wife does need to be kept in the loop on your progress and setbacks, but she is not your accountability partner.

It is vital that you take responsibility for your own recovery. Your wife cannot and should not try to take on that responsibility for you. She can set consequences in your marriage for future failures, but she should not determine what your recovery looks like. You and you alone are fully responsible for that.

You will report your failures to the group and to your wife. But if your wife takes it upon herself to point out every failure that she sees, this will only serve to increase your shame, which will make progress difficult, if not impossible. We will learn in the next lesson how damaging shame can be to our recovery.

> I never assumed one afternoon of confession would fix everything in my relationship with Renee. My actions hurt her deeply. She forgave me, but the emotional wounds wouldn't disappear overnight. Neither would the anger and the doubts and all the other emotions my confession unleashed in her. She needed time to work through them all, and she needed time to learn to trust me again. I told her I had changed, but only time could prove I meant what I said. I had to give it to her. I had to be patient. Very patient.

* If you would like to sign up for Covenant Eyes and benefit Pure Life Alliance at the same time, please use the link found on our homepage: purelifealliance.org.

Without it our relationship could not be rebuilt...It would have been easy to for me to get irritated and yell something like, "I told you I have changed! Why won't you believe me?" But she didn't need that. I had to be calm and without complaining or becoming irritated with her.[4]

—Clay Crosse

ASSIGNMENT

STARTING CONVERSATION WITH YOUR WIFE

Find a time to give your wife the "Give to Your Spouse" handout. Allow her to read it and ask any questions she has.

If you do not know the answer to any of the questions your wife asks, just say you do not know and share these with your mentor at your next meeting. Together you can explore healthy responses that will contribute to the intimacy between you and your wife.

---

[4] Ibid.

LESSON FOUR
Understanding Compulsive Lust

When a man finds himself feeling ensnared or even enslaved by lust, it is important to understand that this did not happen by chance. There is always a history that caused this **compulsive** behavior to develop.

Our History & Vulnerability to Lust

A. Unmet Childhood Needs

Note the diagram on the next page. It demonstrates what happens when a child experiences a need, such as the need for human touch. In the left half of the diagram we see that when a child is in need of something (human touch), he expresses that need and his parents or others around him fill that need (give him affection). This child learns that the world is a safe place and he can rely on others, at least most of the time, to meet needs he cannot meet on his own.

37

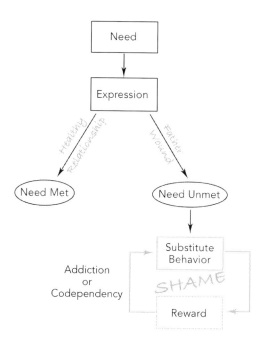

The right side of the diagram shows what happens when needs are not met by others. The child will find a substitute that in some way simulates what it feels like to have that need met. This often results in an addictive or codependent shame cycle.

We find that it is most often a child's father who does not meet the child's needs. This leaves the child feeling wounded by his father and we often refer to this as a **father wound** when a child grows up having to find substitute ways to meet his own needs. Unfortunately, substitutes rarely meet the original need. However, the substitute may offer a reward that approximates getting the need filled.

> Dave remembers the day the wound came. His parents were having an argument in the kitchen, and his father was verbally abusing his mother. Dave took his mom's side, and his father exploded. "I don't remember all that was said, but I do remember his last words: 'You are such a mama's boy,' he yelled at me. Then he walked out."

> Perhaps if Dave had a strong relationship with his dad most of the time, a wound like this might be lessened. But the blow came after years of distance between them. [5]
>
> —John Eldredge

At some point, the child discovers or is shown masturbation and learns that it gives a reward that feels good. It feels sort of like being comforted.

Over time, if the father continues to withhold affection, the boy turns to masturbation as a substitute for real human affection when the need for affection becomes so great he cannot ignore it. It has a reward, but cannot meet the actual need for affection. Unlike real affection, it is not given by another person, it does not offer the same sense of being loved and cared for, and it is done in isolation, not within a loving relationship. In fact, rather than resulting in feeling love, masturbation causes the boy to feel shame and to withdraw further into himself.

Here is a list of some childhood needs that sexual behavior can become a substitute for when they are not met:

- Safety and protection, physically and emotionally
- Human touch
- Physical and emotional nurture
- Mental and physical stimulation
- Being loved for who I am, not what parents want
- Belonging to a healthy extended family
- Security
- Dignity
- Self-worth
- Consistency and predictability in environment
- Honesty and truth from family
- Healthy boundaries for behavior

---

[5] Eldredge, John. *Wild at Heart*. Thomas Nelson, 2001.

- Freedom to make mistakes—not having to be perfect
- Self-determination: to be what I am led to be
- Hope for the future
- Healthy guidance and education about life and relationships

It is important to point out that each of us have had negative experiences related to our parents. This does not make us "different" or inferior; it makes us normal. This is not about blaming our parents or childhood experiences for our current condition. But it can be helpful to understand the roots of our current condition.

> Although they are mostly invisible and often ignored, huge gaping wounds of loneliness and emptiness are afflicting many men and women who attempt to lead meaningful lives…The treatments these wounded ones find in the world are only temporary tonics passed off as cures. They are self-medicating themselves with illusionary relationships, pornographic titillation, idealized fantasies of men and women, fornication, adultery, and masturbation.[6]
>
> —Signa Bodishbaugh

Questions to discuss with your mentor:

- Can you identify any needs that were often not met in your childhood?
- What links do you see in early sexual behavior (pornography, masturbation, etc.) and these unmet needs?

B. Hot-Wired Sexuality

The human brain is not wired to register any interest in sex until after puberty. Sexual arousal, lustful thoughts and interest of any kind in sex that occurs before puberty does not happen naturally. The human body is not programmed to register or even be aware of sexuality before then.

---

[6] Bodishbaugh, Signa. *Illusions of Intimacy* Sovereign World, 2004.

However, some of us did experience arousal before puberty. For some, it is difficult to remember back to a time when we were not keenly aware of sexuality. It is important for us to understand that this only happens when an outside influence introduces us to sex before our brains are capable of dealing with sexuality. Therapists call this hot-wiring our sexuality, or forcing sexual awareness to begin before we are ready for it.

This can occur when someone, even someone our own age, is sexual with us before we reach puberty. This awakens our sexuality early, before we can understand what is happening to us. It can be difficult to define the line between what some may consider normal curiosity and exploration that children sometimes engage in, and sexual behavior that awakens one's sexuality. Rather than debate where that line is, we will simply state that we have found that a high percentage of men who struggle with lust also had sexual experiences as children. Even if the other party was a child of the same age, when the behavior becomes truly sexual it is considered abuse. Research shows in almost all of these cases, the instigating child learned the behavior from someone who abused them or from being exposed to pornography.

Hot-wiring does not have to occur as a result of interaction with others. When children find pornography, especially online video pornography, the same result will occur. Sexuality is introduced and the child will often attempt to replicate what he sees, usually resulting in beginning masturbation long before what would be considered biologically normal.

In either case, the child has found a new way to feel good but also experiences shame afterward. The child will feel drawn to repeating the behavior but ashamed of the behavior at the same time. This destroys self-esteem and begins a life of secrecy and isolation. The fear of being known begins here.

Questions to discuss with your mentor:

- Did you experience any sexual abuse as a child?
- Were you exposed to pornography as a child?

• If so, how did this affect your behavior when you felt the need to be consoled or comforted?

Shame vs. Guilt

This is a good point to stop and explain the difference between shame and guilt. First of all, guilt is mostly good and helpful, while shame is almost always destructive. If we boil it down to the very basic level, here is the difference:

• Guilt is when I feel I have made a mistake.

• Shame is when I feel I am a mistake.

The feeling of guilt is the Holy Spirit's way of telling us we have committed a sin. This is God's warning sign to us to turn around and go the other way. Guilt is God calling us, lovingly, back to Him. Shame, on the other hand, is the feeling that we are, at our core, defective and unacceptable. Shame causes us to run away from God to hide. Guilt comes from God; shame comes from Satan.

The Shame Cycle

It is this kind of history that makes us vulnerable to becoming caught in an endless cycle of shame.

Shame & Isolation

Something happens to cause us to feel shame. It could be someone reprimanding us, failing at a task or feeling rejected. As discussed earlier, our history causes us to withdraw into ourselves when we have these feelings. We isolate ourselves even more when we experience these kinds of negative feelings. We feel ashamed of who we are. Shame gives us thoughts like:

• "I'm not good enough."

• "There's something wrong with me."

• "I'll never measure up."

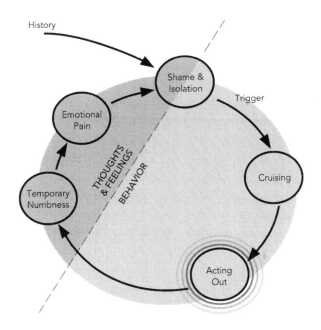

Trigger

These kinds of feelings are called triggers because they lead to an immediate attempt to escape from our feelings of shame.

Cruising

This is when we begin to search for some kind of sexual stimulation because we have previously learned that it soothes our hurts. At this point we probably will not admit to ourselves that we are going to act out sexually, but we put in motion the means to do so. This can be channel surfing, **cruising** the web, deciding to go for a drive that just happens to take us near a porn shop or strip club, or getting alone where no one can watch us. These things we automatically do to put us in a place where we can act out are called **rituals**. They are so ingrained in us we are often completely unaware that we are doing them. This stage can take days, or even weeks—or may be very short. During this stage we may feel that everything reminds us of sex. All we can think about is sex. It is hard to focus on work or even carry on a normal conversation because we are so distracted.

Acting Out

This is when we do something sexual. It could be looking at pornography, masturbating or actually having sexual contact with another person. These behaviors release endorphins in our brains that cause us to feel euphoric and mask over any shame we had been feeling.

Temporary Numbness

Even after **acting out** we sometimes do not feel shame for a while. It is still there, but we have covered it up. However, we are not only numb to shame; we find we are numb to all emotions, even good ones. We may feel somewhat dead inside, blank, unable to experience happiness and joy. Other times, however, we skip this stage entirely.

Emotional Pain

These are feelings of deep regret, such as:

- I really shouldn't have done that.
- I feel miserable and dirty.
- I am not who I wish I could be.

Shame & Isolation

This brings us back full circle to feeling shame for who we are. We have learned not to trust others to help us, so we isolate. We hold on as long as we can, promising ourselves never to act out again, but eventually the shame becomes so great that we are triggered and begin to soothe ourselves by cruising for opportunities to act out.

Living in this endless cycle has taught us to believe things that simply are not true. Some of them are:

- Acting out will make be feel better.
- Sex is my most important need.

- If I can find just the right pornographic image or video, if I can create the perfect fantasy, if I can have the right sexual experience, I will finally be happy.
- If I can figure out how, I can stop this acting out on my own.
- If anyone truly knew me, they would not love me.

None of the above beliefs are true. None of them are even partially true. Sex cannot make us happy. Lust only grows stronger the more we chase it. Our emptiness actually has nothing to do with sex. We will never be able to escape this spiral of shame on our own. And if we did let someone really know us we would, perhaps for the first time, experience real love.

These are hard beliefs to change, but the journey out of endless lust requires us to reshape the false beliefs we have embraced.

Escalating Acting Out

In the beginning, we often draw a line that we promise ourselves not to cross. This is our way of compromising with our conscience. "Well, I'll look at porn this time, but only soft-porn." Unfortunately, we usually find over time that staying behind the line we draw no longer covers up shame like it used to. We move the line farther away and indulge in more serious forms of acting out in order to get the same sense of escape and euphoria.

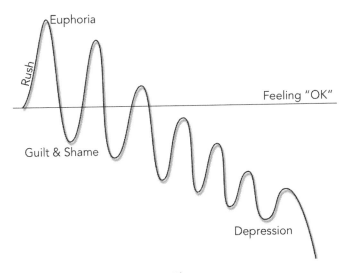

45

In other words, the frequency and/or severity of our acting out increases over time.

Of course, our increased levels of acting out cause us to feel even more shame, which simply drives us into the next round more quickly. We begin to feel truly trapped in this cycle of lust and shame.

This is what the Bible talks about when it uses the phrase *a slave to sin*. We find ourselves trapped in a cycle we cannot escape from. "Jesus replied, 'I tell you the truth, everyone who sins is a slave to sin.'" — John 8:34

> The euphoric experiences of sexual and chemical highs wear off, and more stimulation is needed to get that same high. Every successive use or experience increases our tolerance to sex and chemicals...As lust grows, more stimulation is required to quench it...As the decline continues, a sexual habit brings an increasing dependency on the experience. The euphoria becomes a means of releasing stress and tension. The mind is filled with pornographic images and the memory of actual experiences. Many people in sexual bondage begin to withdraw from others and from God as the degradation continues. [7]
>
> —Neil Anderson

In the end, no matter what we do, we cannot recapture the euphoria we once experienced. In fact, we cannot even get back to feeling normal. Depression can become our normal state.

Before we get too depressed about being depressed, it is important to know that there really is a way off this not-so-merry-go-round. That is in the next lesson! For now, let's stop and identify how this is currently playing out in our lives.

---

[7] Anderson, Neil. *Winning the Battle Within.* Harvest House Publishers, 2008.

ASSIGNMENT

DESCRIBING THE STRUGGLE

Answer the following and share with your mentor:

What things have you tried to stop acting out that have not worked?

What are some of your triggers? That is, what are things that cause you to feel shame when they occur?

Re-read the section on "Cruising" on page 43. What parts of this description do you see happening in your own life? Be very specific.

Can you identify any instinctive rituals you have that lead you to act out?

Describe how your acting out has escalated either in frequency or severity over time.

ASSIGNMENT

BEGIN A JOURNAL

Yes, we know that many men do not like even the idea of journaling, but it is very helpful. Begin a daily journal that you keep which you will only share with your mentor or accountability group.

Make an entry every day.

Try to think of anything that happened during the day that you feel embarrassed about, angry about or ashamed of. Write a brief description of each.

 Share these with your mentor the next time you meet.

ASSIGNMENT

CREATE A SUBSTITUTIONS LIST

As you have learned in this lesson, most of the time our "acting out" is really an attempt to fill a need that is not really sexual. Even after understanding this, we still experience the desire to act out when we're triggered.

Write a short list of things you can substitute for acting out. These should be things that actually come closer to meeting the real need you have. They should be things you enjoy, but are healthy. This could include things like going for a walk, reading a book, having a cup of coffee, calling a friend, listening to music, playing music, writing a love note to your wife, doing a hobby and so on.

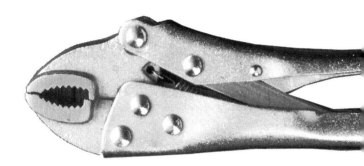

LESSON FIVE
Masturbation

Few topics stir up as much controversy as that of masturbation. It is one of the earliest and most personal forms of sexual sin many men experience. This seemingly private act affects our relationships with everyone around us, including our wives, families and friends. Many well-known authors, including Drs. Mark Laaser and Doug Weiss, talk about how it ruins our sex lives and steals **intimacy** from an addict's spouse. More than that, it certainly colors our relationship with God.

In this lesson, we will consider misconceptions about masturbation, its negative impact and the positive outcomes that result from stopping this all-too-familiar habit.

How Can Self-Sex Be So Unhealthy?

For most sexual addicts, masturbation is a solitary behavior. It isolates you from your wife. The impact of this is less intimacy, not more. For example, if you masturbate to achieve half of your orgasms, you are excluding her from half of your sexual energy. And she is receiving only half the sexual attention you have to offer her. It's not a stretch to view this as a form of neglect.

> Marital sex is not for the purpose of satisfying selfish desires. If that is all we are doing, we will never be satisfied. [8]
>
> —Mark Laaser

Mutually enthusiastic, satisfying sexual attention between you and your wife is one of the most important bonding experiences. When we think about it in our right mind, why would we turn our back on such a powerful opportunity? In effect, your own hand is stealing time, intimacy and marital satisfaction from your wife.

You likely have become conditioned to the ritual and to the method you use to masturbate. There is automatic feedback associated with self-stimulation so that the pleasurable experience is maximized. It is possible for you to prefer masturbation (an artificial relationship experience) over the actual experience of making love to your wife. This is a dangerous situation, and is the basis for the claim that masturbation ruins sex lives. It deprives your wife of your sexual availability, but more than that it has reframed your perception of your sexuality. It fuels the false belief that sex is all about your gratification. This could not be further from the truth. Sexual intimacy is meant to be an expression of an emotional and spiritual intimacy shared between a man and his wife.

For a single man, masturbation may be his primary means of sexual fulfillment. However, we believe that all sexual activity is reserved for marriage. God forbids sexual activity outside of marriage, since to do so is at the very least lusting after someone you who does not belong to you. Earl Wilson, author and sexual addiction therapist, encourages men to use the mental mantra, "She is none of my business!"

God enables our bodies to meet real physical needs through ejaculation while asleep (wet dreams). By masturbation, we literally take things into

---

[8]Laaser, Mark. "Masturbation: The Secret That Ruins Great Sex." *New Man Magazine,* July/August 2000.

our own hands, saying to God, "I don't trust your plans for me; I don't need you; I can take care of myself." For single men, sexual intimacy is a blessing that God potentially has for you in the future. Trust Him in this and He will bless you.

Similarly dangerous is the type of fantasy in which people receive virtual nurturing. All men and women need to be valued and loved through nurturing care. Receiving this care through fantasy such as a chat room, a phone call, a picture image or an imagined partner offers a cheap replacement for engaging with your wife to meet your sexual needs. Needless to say, these sources of pseudo-intimacy are false and lead to isolation and disappointment.

Finally, when we masturbate, what are we thinking about? The Bible is clear about lustful fantasy. In Matthew 5:27-28, we are taught that lustful thoughts about another partner constitute adultery. This is equally true for erotic images that evoke these thoughts.

In the light of day, we might choose instead to seek the mutually nurturing, actual relationship-enhancing behavior of spousal intimacy as God intended. This, of course, demonstrates a clear, truthful view of sexual intimacy with your wife.

Perceived Benefits vs. Risks

Comparing some of the perceived benefits of masturbating with some of the risks is a helpful exercise; one that very few sexual addicts are willing to explore. As addicts we often find ourselves in a place of denial and delusion. To truly examine the act of masturbating requires discipline, maturity and personal responsibility. These are three characteristics you likely believe are lacking in your life. You may have believed this lesson was only helping with your habitual masturbation, but instead it is also teaching you to think more critically about this and other related issues in your life.

The chart on the next page illustrates a small number of benefits and risks to consider. As you read through these, think about how each of them has

BENEFITS (perceived)	RISKS
It gives a good physical feeling due to a chemical rush.	It creates guilt and often leads to a sense of failure.
It allows the avoidance of some painful realities through fantasy.	It can create the impression that sexual release is a necessary function.
It provides the transient experience of being a virtual center of attention.	It can make one believe that problems are solved or do not exist.
	It leads to a disconnection from God, spouses and friends.
	It can contribute to a false sense of self-esteem.

impacted your decisions about masturbation. Each point will move you further down the road to freedom from masturbation, but only if you honestly engage these truths.

If you are unwilling to ponder this list, giving it serious consideration, we would suggest you question your readiness to heal from your sexual addiction. Resist the urge to rush quickly through these. Instead, focus on each item with an open heart and mind, and discuss your thoughts with your mentor.

ASSIGNMENT

MAKE A LIST

 Make your own list of what you get from masturbation, as well as what you lose. Discuss this list with your mentor.

Some Thoughts Toward Stopping

If you have a long-established habit of masturbating, it is probably not realistic to stop overnight. Consider setting a goal, which is a step ahead of where you are. Make this goal a part of your accountability line.

There are many ways to approach stopping a habit of masturbating. Some believe it is solely an issue of determination and willpower: if you have not been able to stop it is because you are not determined enough or submissive enough to God's plan for your life. These types of approaches tend to pile on additional shame. Your shame pile is already large enough; feeling badly about your inability to just plain stop masturbating will ultimately leave you wanting to masturbate more.

So what is a more healthy approach? A method that makes lasting change addresses the reasons why you masturbate. The motives that drive you to repeatedly masturbate must be discovered. The "benefits" in the chart on the opposite page are included in this category.

On the other side of the discussion is your positive motivations to stop. Spend some time discussing with your mentor some good things that will come from no longer masturbating. Here are just a few for you to consider:

- I am committed to my wife, and want that person to have 100% of my sexuality.

- I don't want to become habituated to self-stimulation, rendering spousal relations dissatisfying.

- I want to uphold the personal principles by which I live, including living my life with the end in mind.

Since it is clear we view masturbation as a solution, then what might be the problem being solved? It could be a relationship issue, spiritual disconnectedness, self-esteem issues, shyness, entitlement or any number of other needs that aren't being met through healthier means. When you are committed to stopping masturbation, you will find a willingness to be purposeful and thoughtful in your solutions. This is more easily said than done. A crucial thought process you must adopt is often called "mindfulness." Some believe the concept of being mindful of yourself and others is a concept from Buddhism. However, in a passage written by the Apostle Paul, we see a commandment to be very aware of ourselves and those around us.

> Everyone should look out not only for his own interests, but also for the interests of others.
> —Philippians 2:4

This is the Biblical "mindfulness" we are instructed to apply. And it's a powerful approach to understanding our motivations to masturbate. When you're being tempted to masturbate, stop everything and ask yourself these questions:

- What are my current needs?
- What have I been thinking about?
- What feelings have I been experiencing during the last few days and/or hours?

In Steve Gallagher's book *At the Altar of Sexual Idolatry*, Paul is again quoted—this time regarding the impact of salvation in a man's life. Whereas before conversion, most decisions were made with the intention of satisfying a man's natural desires, now he is imparted with a whole new value system. But the physical longings of the flesh are still relentless. Thus Paul agonizes over this struggle: "For the flesh sets its desire against the Spirit, and the Spirit against the flesh; for these are in opposition to one another, so that you may not do the things that you please" (Gal 5:17). There was no war previously because the flesh enjoyed total freedom in its influence.

Masturbation may be a manifestation of pride, in that we choose to do what seems to be pleasing to our human flesh instead of what is pleasing to God. When we place something ahead of God in our lives, it can be a form of idolatry, and we must be vigilantly aware of it.

Finally, when we are aware of our need to change, our first steps toward that change are possible. When you—as a married or single person—realize that a Christ-centered life does not include the pattern of masturbation, you are then able to begin the process of stopping. We believe that all men must work toward being free of masturbation. For some it is possible to take an all-or-nothing, cold-turkey approach, and for others, as we have said, this may not happen overnight. Regardless, we would strongly encourage you to consider it a journey toward healthy sexuality. Whichever way works for you, be careful to not mix shame into an already-difficult process of making better choices with your sexuality.

ASSIGNMENT

BREAKING THE HABIT

Discuss with your mentor what you will incorporate into your accountability line that demonstrates a healthy engagement in breaking free from a habit of masturbation.

LESSON SIX
Restoring Intimacy

Over the long haul, since God has made us sexual creatures, it is crucial that we build a healthy view of sexuality as part of the healing journey. As men, this is something we must pursue with the same effort we use to avoid sexual sin. What you are about to read is not something you can accomplish during the next week, month or even year. But we want to equip you to approach this topic well, right now and for the coming season.

If you are a married man, be assured you are not going to enjoy this lesson. If you are a single man, you may be tempted to skip to the next lesson. After all, you are not married. But this would be a mistake as this chapter will begin re-crafting your understanding of your sexuality. Whether married or single, be brave and read on. You will be glad you did… eventually.

Real intimacy is only achievable when we have empathy for our significant other. Many of our wives were hurt and wounded in this area—largely due to incorrect beliefs and expectations—even before they found out about our sexual addiction. If you are a part of a Pure Life Alliance FMO group, it is likely your sex life was not even healthy before "the issue" came out.

As unfortunate as it may be, many couples have never had good instruction on what healthy sexuality looks like. We often talk about sexual issues in the heat of the moment—which is typically not a good time for difficult conversation topics.

Adding to an already shaky situation, when it is discovered—or we finally disclose our sexual behavior—our wives immediately wonder if they are physically safe...even from disease. They do not feel mentally or emotionally safe and have little desire to be exposed or vulnerable with us. Even amidst this tension, wives often hold a false belief that if they do not agree to have sex with us, we will just go elsewhere for it. Read this next sentence carefully: Nothing could be further from the truth. Your wife's sexual unavailability is not the problem; therefore her sexual availability is not the solution.

"More Sex, Please"

You may believe the answer to sexual sin is to have more sex with your wife. The reasoning goes: If a man has that much desire to be sexual, his wife simply needs to meet these needs. A spiritual leader might even justify this view by quoting Scripture.

Unfortunately, well-intentioned pastors have inflicted much harm and spiritual abuse to wives who have already been wounded by their husband's infidelity. We will discuss a more healthy application of Scripture through Paul's words further in this lesson. For now, suffice it to say—more sex is not the path to healthy sexual intimacy.

Whatever we do, whether it happens to be a physical or mental accomplishment, it takes hard work with much practice, sacrifice and purposefulness. A pianist plays a technical and beautiful piece only after hundreds of hours of practice. A professional basketball player excels at scoring for his team after thousands of practices and working on the

https://youtu.be/loZ8CBCv2uQ

fundamentals of the game. Some might argue that working on a healthy marriage is more difficult than these illustrations, and they would be right!

This reality is true of our most intimate https://youtu.be/wyeO8WCgTjU relationships. Our culture has convinced us that sex is an experience any two consenting people can share and this act will meet their needs. Recently a popular prime time show portrayed this lie. Two people had been dating for five weeks and the woman character was expressing frustration that they had not yet had sex. She says, "It's been more than a month and we haven't made love. Is something wrong?" The back-story is that he sleeps around, but believes she may be "the one." He is hesitant to follow a familiar path with her. Presumably, he wants to build a healthy relationship and not jump right to sex. While the creators of the show and the actor himself would not make the claim that marriage should come before sex, clearly there is a natural order to developing intimacy.

sex

marriage

love

respect

trust

values

The Bible tells us that sexual intimacy must remain in a marriage relationship occurring between a man and a woman. It also includes an expectation that both husbands and wives love and respect each other. Further, through mutual submission, they prove that trust has been established in their relationship.

Values, trust, respect, love and marriage are needed precursors to sexual intimacy. These are the kinds of things that make sex a natural outcome. Your sexual addiction has undermined and caused cracks in each of these building blocks. In fact, it is likely you have never really had truly healthy views of any of these elements. And in all probability, whole portions of these prerequisites for lovemaking are broken in your marriage. They need to be rebuilt.

Your desire to make love with your wife is healthy when it is an outflowing of shared values, a mutual trust and respect, and a sacrificial love. This is a goal for which to strive. This is what will bring a deep and abiding solution to your sexual addiction. More sex with your wife is not the answer. The satisfying answer for both you and your wife is healthy sex based on this foundation. If we do not choose to invest in these building blocks, our foundation for sex will be dangerously cracked and broken.

Two Lies About Sex

While there are more lies about sex offered by many sources, the two we will discuss will equip you well for this next portion of your journey. And fortunately, God's Word has much to say about our sexuality. The two truths below can strengthen your purity journey if you choose to believe His Word.

Lie #1: My Body Is My Own

This particular lie finds its roots back in the garden of Eden. As Eve heard the enemy's message ("Did God really say?!"), she was encouraged to question God's good intent for her. The enemy convinced her to doubt God's promises and instruction.

> Before sex can be rewarding for both partners, they have to first restore the ability to confide and reestablish emotional openness, to establish a sense of camaraderie. Then physical closeness has meaning, and the meaning serves only to heighten the pleasure of the physical experience even more. [9]
>
> — Lori H. Gordon

As a married man, the lie that says "my body is my own" has at its source the belief that we must take care of ourselves. It tells us that no one, including God, will care for our needs the way we need them to be addressed. It fuels a self-centric attitude that I as an individual am ultimately most important. This then moves us to the belief that others are not as important as I am. And finally, it causes us to value others based on

---

[9] Gordon, Lori H. "Intimacy: The Art of Relationships, How Relationships Are Sabotaged by Hidden Expectations." *Psychology Today,* December 31, 1969.

their willingness or ability to meet our needs.

How will you know if this lie has taken hold in your life? If you are honest with yourself, it is quite easy to tell. If having an orgasm has become your highest relational goal with your wife, you are living this lie. When this lie informs how you relate to your wife sexually, it is a recipe for disaster. It views her as a means to an end—that end being sexual satisfaction at the cost of deepening trust, love and security.

ASSIGNMENT

GETTING A CLEARER VIEW

What should you do now? The graphic on p.59 shows the foundation that sex must rest on if it is to be healthy. Look again at that image.

Are there ways you have undermined her trust in you?

Do you feel at times disrespected by her? If so, in what ways might you address that with her?

Are there physical ways you can express your love that are not always preceding an expectation of sexual intimacy?

Consider trusting your wife with a personal, emotional struggle you have been afraid to share.

Encourage her to read this lesson. Intimacy is a shared experience. If she learns what you are learning about restoring intimacy, you can walk this part of the journey together.

You might express a willingness to wait until she is ready to be sexually intimate with you. But only make this commitment if you truly are willing to wait; do not use this to manipulate her into trusting you more.

Ultimately a Biblical view of who owns your body is most critical. What does God say about your body? Two of the clearest passages on this topic are found in Paul's first letter to the Corinthians.

Paul says in 1 Corinthians 6:20, "…for God bought you with a high price. So you must honor God with your body." This passage talks in detail about running from sexual sin.

ASSIGNMENT

I AM BOUGHT, NOW WHAT?

Spend some quiet time considering the implications of what it means to be owned by God. Look up and read through 1 Corinthians 6. If you have made Jesus your Lord, verses 9-20 of this chapter link your relationship with Him to motivation to live in a pure way.

In a broader context of marriage, Paul addresses the mutual ownership of the bodies of both the husband and wife.

> The wife's body does not belong to her alone but also to her husband. In the same way, the husband's body does not belong to him alone but also to his wife.
>
> —1 Corinthians 7:4

The lie that your body is your own—and you may do whatever you please with it—stands in direct conflict to this Biblical truth. If you wish to restore a healthy sexual relationship with your spouse, you must honor the ownership your wife has of your body. You do not get to use your body for your own pleasure apart from relationship with your wife. When or if you do, you leave yourself open to profound sexual sin and brokenness.

Lie #2: Sexual Intimacy Can Happen Apart From Emotional Intimacy

From the pornography you have viewed to the latest James Bond film to the tabloid headlines in the grocery store, our culture tells us sex is a pleasure to have with any willing partner. This lie says that sex is an end in itself. There is no need to see it in the context of a larger understanding of human intimacy. It is an activity whose purpose is to be experienced in the present; emotional intimacy is not needed for physical fulfillment.

If you are a Christian you likely responded to the previous paragraph with a mixture of disdain and shame. The part of you that believes what God says about sexual purity crafts the disdain in your mind. "How can the world be so wrong about sex?" you may ask yourself. Or you may make statements like, "It's so sad to see how twisted our culture is becoming and how broken our view of sex has become." These are perspectives that are informed by your faith. They are the outworking of your set of beliefs founded on your Christian faith. But, unfortunately for you, they have not informed your sexual choices. While you profess disgust with the over-sexualization of our culture, there is also a strong pull that has forced you to compartmentalize your behavior from your beliefs.

This is where your sense of shame resides. You want this type of sex to be "morally right" to condone indiscriminate sex with whomever you please, but your soul cries out against the lie. It is here that you find yourself caught in the dichotomy crafted by the distance between your worldview and your actions.

Think carefully about this truism: believe the behavior. Your behavior finds its source in what you actually believe. That is, if your sexual actions match the world's, so does your belief about your sexuality. The shame you carry, because this is true, provides a foothold for living out Lie #2. While few would either admit to or be able to identify this dynamic in themselves, many Christians live with these mutually exclusive views. So you are not alone in this.

However, you must be ruthless in your effort to root out this lie. Your work as a man struggling with sexual sin is to honestly pursue any hint of sexual impurity, making all efforts to put it to death.

> But sexual immorality and any impurity or greed should not even be heard of among you, as is proper for saints. Coarse and foolish talking or crude joking are not suitable, but rather giving thanks.
> — Ephesians 5:3,4

This lie that sexual intimacy can happen apart from emotional intimacy is one such impurity. As long as you believe these views are mutually inclusive, you will find yourself using your sexuality for your own purpose. Do not settle for this. Purity is not just about stopping your behavior. Purity envelops your whole being: mind, body and soul.

When you find yourself being tempted to act on this lie, call it what it is. "This is a lie!" Then pick up the phone and call your mentor. With more practice you will be able to identify this lie sooner. This is the process of being more pure as you continue to find greater alignment between what you believe and what you do. This is the process of correcting your view of sexual intimacy and its purpose. So be encouraged, stay focused and keep on track!

Using The Sexual Agreement...When You're Ready

The concept of the sexual agreement, provided by Doug Weiss, is one example of a healthy way to restore sexual intimacy with your wife. When both spouses agree to use it, this tool can be really powerful.

However, the reverse is true as well. If one spouse is committed to a sexual agreement while the other is not, it can be perceived as a forced intimacy or—even worse—a way to manipulate your wife to meet your physical needs and an attempt to bypass her emotional needs. To this point, you have not shown yourself to be a reliable partner, particularly in this most intimate area, so it will take time for your wife to enter into another agreement with you. If your wife is resistant, express an interest in talking more about it two or three months from now. Then mark your calendar and be faithful to discuss it again when the time is right...not before. This gives you ample time to pray and practice the "Three Dailies."

We will not discuss the "Three Dailies" at length here, but Weiss strongly recommends practicing them for 60 to 90 days before implementing the sexual agreement. These include prayer, discussing feelings, and praising and nurturing your wife. For more on these, read p. 147 of "Sex, Men & God" and view the short videos on praying with your wife and our role as husbands in praising our wives.

https://youtu.be/4X9rnDIz5Jo   https://youtu.be/Hjy2yK0nz5A

You should expect more support on sexual intimacy when you and a mentor work through *Solid Foundation: A Mentored Guide to Continue Building Your Purity, Module Two.*

LESSON SEVEN
Leaving the Cycle

First of all, let's begin by reminding ourselves of one of the lies we must denounce: *If I can only figure out how, I can stop this acting out on my own.* Compulsive lust is impossible to break free from alone. We are, in fact, powerless to escape it.

Fortunately, God designed an off-ramp to get us out of this endless cycle of shame and lust. To break this cycle we must address shame. It is shame, not lust, that drives this cycle and it is shame that we must focus on.

The key to removing shame in our lives is a commitment to no longer keeping secrets. We need to share the things we feel shame about with others we can trust. You will find huge relief in coming out of isolation and sharing your secrets.

> Therefore, confess your sins to one another and pray for one another, so that you may be healed. The urgent request of a righteous person is very powerful in its effect.
>
> —James 5:16

Point Out What Is Shaming You

Beyond any sexual sin we have committed, we have plenty of other things that cause us shame. These are the things that caused us shame before we ever started committing sexual sins. Things like failures and feelings of rejection. Share these with others and together we will learn to identify things we have felt shame about that we can let go of and no longer feel bad about.

Reject Satan's Lies

When we experience feelings of shame due to our failures, we will likely feel shame. After we become aware of what is happening in our minds, we must reject the lies we have come to believe. The lies that tell us we are not acceptable. The lies that tell us we are a mistake. These are lies that Satan whispers into our minds. We can actually stop and tell Satan to stop lying to us. We can call our trusted friends and tell them what we were beginning to feel to get encouragement to not believe them. We can remind ourselves of the truths from God.

> What then? Should we sin because we are not under law but under grace? Absolutely not!
>
> —Romans 6:14

> If we confess our sins, He is faithful and righteous to forgive us our sins and to cleanse us from all unrighteousness.
>
> —1 John 1:9

> For God did not send His Son into the world that He might condemn the world, but that the world might be saved through Him. Anyone who believes in Him is not condemned...
>
> —John 3:17-18

God loves you; He does not condemn you. Even when we blatantly sin, He forgives us. When we are at work or home and try to do something and fail, that is not even a sin. There is no reason to even feel guilt in this situation, much less shame. God tells us to talk to others about the things that shame us. Then we can learn to see when we are feeling shame, and reject it. Let others help you see where you are holding onto shame; shame that you can let go.

Essentially, this means we need to have close relationships with other men who we can trust to talk about all this with. We will still feel shame for a while, but when we do, we now have a different route to take rather than turning to lust. We have an off-ramp: reaching out to trusted men.

> I realize that this level of relationship is threatening to most men, but the need is still there. No one understands men like another man. Yes, women have a unique place in our lives, but they can't call out our masculinity in the way another male can...they lack the ability to speak to a man's façades with a man's language.
>
> Though men do not do this naturally (and we are socialized not to), I suggest it is God's will. What did Peter mean when he said, "Above all, love each other deeply" (1 Peter 4:8)? Was he talking about opposite sex relationships? If he was talking about men loving men, surely it was intended to go beyond Super Bowl parties and prayer breakfasts. [10]
>
> —Russell Willingham

At first, this will feel awkward. But for the first time we will begin to feel as if we are truly known...because we are! As we share parts of our lives that we have always kept hidden, and then experience not just acceptance, but love, we begin to experience what intimacy is. Not sexual intimacy, but relational intimacy. And only relational intimacy can truly help ease and remove our feelings of shame.

Yes, life will go on and there will be times when we begin to feel inadequate again. And for quite some time this may lead us back to feeling shame and wanting to isolate from others. But, if we dare to reach out again and share our painful feelings with our new trusted brothers, those feelings of shame will diminish.

---

[10] Willingham, Russell. *Breaking Free.* InterVarsity Press, 1999.

There will still be temptation to return to pornography, fantasy and masturbation. Those are deeply imprinted into our brains and we return to them as if on auto-pilot. While simply trying harder never works, we will have times we must use our willpower to resist these temptations. We have to surrender our right to enjoy the pleasures of lust so that we can learn to enjoy the greater pleasure of relational intimacy. It takes a while to convince ourselves that real relationships are better than imaginary ones. We must put up some roadblocks to help us resist temptation.

ASSIGNMENT

Create Your Plan

Review your Accountability Line that you created in Lesson Two. The plan you are creating should be designed to help you avoid doing the things on your Away from Impurity list.

> Accountability groups and relationships will remind us of many truths. One of them is that God loves us no matter what we've done or who we've become. An accountability group reminds us we are liked, even with all our sinful behaviors. Finally, an accountability group reminds us that we need to trust, take risks, and surrender control of how others think about us. In short, accountability encourages us to tell the truth. [11]
>
> —Mark Laaser

List the names of any people that you need to avoid for a while who are bad influences when it comes to your struggle to avoid lust.

List any parts of town that take you near places where you have had non-marital sexual experiences or spent money on pornography or other sex-related services. This may include stores that have magazines that cause you to feel aroused, or any place that causes you to feel aroused.

What is your plan to make the Internet safe for you?

---

[11] Laaser, Mark. *The 7 Principles of Highly Accountable Men.* Beacon Hill Press, 2011.

HALT–SOS

Consider the acronym: HALT–SOS. You will be more vulnerable when you are Hungry, Angry, Lonely, Tired, Stressed, Overwhelmed or Sick. When you do experience a trigger that you could not anticipate or that you failed to avoid, you will need to already have a plan in place. Stop what you are doing (HALT) and reach out for help (SOS). This acronym helps you be aware of vulnerable times and reminds you of what to do during a dangerous window of temptation.

As we slide toward the Cruising stage our minds become preoccupied with sex, disrupting our mental thought patterns. It is as if a fog begins to set in.

> One night my friend Andrew and I went to rent a video. At the door to the video store he stopped and said, "I'll wait out here." "Why," I asked. "I don't want to go in," he said. He explained that God had convicted him about looking at the explicit covers of many videos. His way of fighting back was not even to enter.
>
> A lot of people can admit that lust is a prevalent sin in their life and say they want to change. But unlike Andrew, they've never taken the time to think through how the process of temptation unfolds for them. Instead of anticipating and being on their guard, they're surprised by the same attack over and over. I've been guilty of this myself. [12]
>
> —Joshua Harris

Make a list now of what you will do whenever you are triggered or feel yourself becoming hungry, angry, lonely, tired, stressed, overwhelmed or sick. Ideas include calling a trusted friend immediately, thinking about what you like about your wife, reminding yourself that these feelings will pass and are not permanent, reading Scriptures that remind you of God's love, and reading your "Letter to Myself."

---

[12] Harris, Joshua. *Sex Is Not the Problem (Lust Is)*. Multnomah Books, 2003.

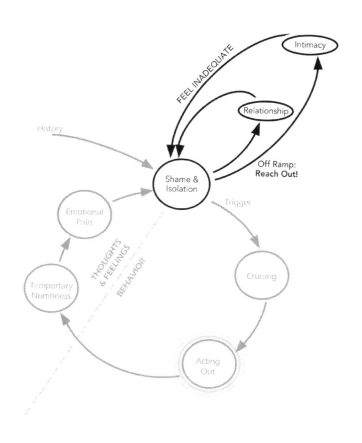

Things To Consider

Be wary of alcohol; it greatly reduces our self-control. This may be a time to avoid drinking for a while. Be aware of your tendency to simply switch ways of medicating pain. Things like compulsive eating, drinking, drug use, sports, TV, shopping, working, thrill-seeking or other mood-altering behaviors are only ways to avoid feeling and do not help us.

Becoming more religious is sometimes a way people try to cover up feelings of shame, but this is not what God wants from us, either, and it is not helpful.

Trying to control others can also be something people turn to when giving up chasing after lust. These things do not feel as bad on the surface to us, but all of them are simply other ways of avoiding dealing with shame. Only vulnerability before God and trusted others removes shame.

Finally, be gentle with yourself. Change this deep takes time. None of us will succeed as quickly as we wish. God is our example in His patience with us; we should be patient with each other and ourselves.

LESSON EIGHT
Review of Module One

The purpose of this lesson is to review what you have learned and to find ways to use it to help you continue your journey of recovery.

Lesson 1 – It's a Journey, Not a Destination

What value did writing your story have for you?

List some of the damage caused by your sexual sin.

Lesson 2 – Facing the Past, Finding Hope for the Future

What role did denial and delusion play in your ongoing sexual behavior?

List some of the things you have tried attempting to stop this behavior.

What will happen if you do not get this sin under control?

Lesson 3 – Disclosure and Rebuilding Trust

What should you disclose, and to whom?

Who should you probably not disclose to?

Why are the three steps to rebuilding trust (sincerity, ability, durability) important for your wife?

Lesson 4 – Understanding Compulsive Lust

In your particular case, what things played into the formation of your sexual sin?

What is shame, and how did you come to feel it?

What are your rituals?

What does acting out look like in your life?

What things can you do to begin reducing feelings of shame in your life?

Lesson 5 – Masturbation

Do you agree that masturbation ruins your sex life? Why or why not?

Name a risk of masturbating that really impacted you. Why was this particular risk difficult for you?

What is your next-step goal toward stopping masturbation? Is it on your accountability line?

Lesson 6 – Restoring Intimacy

If your wife had more sex with you, would this solve your addiction problem? Why or why not?

Which of the five needed precursors to sexual intimacy do you find most difficult? Why?

Describe why having your sexual needs met by your wife is a more fulfilling experience than your sexual sin.

Choose one thing you plan to do for your wife which will invest in non-sexual intimacy. On a scale of 1–10, how committed are you to loving her in this way?

Lesson 7 – Leaving the Cycle

What are the things you will try to stop doing as listed on your Accountability Line?

What need have you been using these things to meet?

What things can you keep away from altogether that will help you avoid being triggered?

What are four things on your substitution list that you can do rather than act out?

What are you willing (or not willing) to do in order to be free from this slavery to sexual sin?

Can you trust God that what is before you is better than what is behind you? This is called hope, to desire with expectation of fulfillment. God is good and he loves you more than anyone; and his desire for you is that you find total satisfaction in him alone. Whatever secrets you are hiding, whatever dividedness you are experiencing in your life, any pain or abuse or shame you carry, God can heal it. You may think it would be impossible for your life to be free from shame or secrets or self, but with God all things are possible. [13]

—Jonathan Daugherty

[13] Daugherty, Jonathan. *Secrets.* Tate Publishing, 2009.

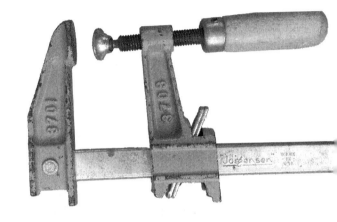

APPENDICES

APPENDIX A
Dealing with Disclosure

Many questions we receive in our For Men Only, Hidden Hurt and Transparent Love groups pertain to disclosure, so we thought it might be helpful to address some of those here.

What is disclosure and how do we do it?

When we talk about disclosure we are referring to the process in which a person struggling with sexual addiction tells others about his/her sexual behaviors. Although there are many scenarios in which a persons' sexual behaviors outside of the marriage might be discovered and confronted, we believe it is important to have a formal time of disclosure between addict and spouse that is planned and in a safe place.

Guidelines for disclosure we generally suggest to couples in recovery:

- The addict works with a counselor or mentor in his small group to create a timeline of all of his sexual behaviors beginning with childhood and ending with the present. (The timeline includes any sexual abuse, first sexual experiences, as well as acting out behaviors before and after marriage.)

- When the struggler is confident that the timeline of sexual experiences/ behaviors is complete, he and the counselor/mentor talk about what needs to be shared with the spouse, what may be shared with the spouse, and what details need to be avoided during disclosure.

- A formal time of disclosure is planned with the spouse when the couple can meet together in a safe place. We do not recommend a restaurant as a safe place due to the public environment. This can prohibit or inhibit freedom in sharing or responding on the part of either the addict or the spouse.

- During the time of disclosure the addict discloses the extent of his sexual behaviors while the spouse listens.

- After disclosure the spouse is allowed to respond and ask clarifying questions.

What do I need to know about my spouse's sexual behaviors?

What is shared during a time of formal disclosure is very important. There are some things that absolutely must be shared in order for healing to take place in the marriage. There are other things that may be shared if the struggler feels safe enough to do so. And there are details about sexual behaviors that should not be shared with a spouse. Let's talk about what these look like.

Examples of sexual behaviors that need to be disclosed:

- Use of pornography in any form – Internet, magazines, videos, etc.

- If the pornography is outside the "norm" (e.g. same-sex, cross-dressing, bondage, bestiality, etc.), then that information should be shared with the spouse. Names of exact websites should NOT be given. One way to think about this is, "If my spouse came across the websites or images I viewed later, would she have a legitimate right to feel that I had not shared fully?" Another way of thinking about this is, after disclosure, is the struggler still afraid of being "found out"?

- Compulsive masturbation

- Sexual behaviors that involved other people – intercourse, oral sex, lap dances, etc.

- Types of sexual encounters – anonymous encounters, one-night stands, prostitutes, short- or long-term affairs, massages, phone sex, cyber sex, etc.

- Names of affair partners that the spouse knows or is acquainted with – friend, co-worker, church member.

- Any behaviors that facilitated sexual encounters – placing personal ads, chatting online, going to strip clubs or bars, etc.

- Any sexual behaviors that resulted in pregnancies, abortions or children.
- Any illegal sexual behaviors – voyeurism, exhibitionism, etc.
- Any financial and/or legal consequences of which a spouse is unaware.
- Any physical consequences of which a spouse is unaware (e.g. contraction of an STD).
- Sexual involvement with children or minors

Examples of sexual behaviors that may be disclosed:

- Sexual abuse experienced as a child.
- Sexual behaviors and encounters that happened before engagement/ marriage.

Examples of details to avoid during disclosure:

- Specific websites the addict frequented.
- Specific times/places where sexual encounters occurred.
- Names of partners spouse does not know.
- Details about the sexual encounter—what a person was wearing, physical characteristics of the partner, what was done together, what was said, etc.

But I want to know everything. Why shouldn't I know all the details?

We know how difficult it is when you first learn about your spouse's betrayal. You want to make sense of it all, and a million questions swirl around in your head. Please understand: knowing details about your spouse's sexual behaviors will end up hurting you. Details help us to picture or visualize our spouse doing or participating in sexual behaviors with others. The more details we know about our spouse's experiences, the harder it will be for us to let go of the hurt and pain and move through the grieving process. Details make things more real and more powerful. When we picture something in our minds, the emotional impact is much greater. Do not seek to know details about all that your spouse has done. You will have enough to grieve as it is. And don't forget that you can talk to your small group about your fears and concerns. Those further along on the journey will be able to help you during this difficult time.

What questions should I ask?

There are some good questions to ask your spouse after he discloses. Let us share some examples of those kinds of questions with you.

You can check out intuitions/suspicions you had at the time. (So, that night when I caught you on the computer at 2 a.m. you were looking at porn?)

You can ask how the addiction has impacted your spouse's relationship with you. (Is this the reason we haven't had sex in three months?)

You can ask about how the addiction has impacted your family's finances. (How much of our money have you spent acting out sexually?)

You can ask about consequences of sexual behaviors that impact you. (Did you have unprotected sex?)

You can address any fears you have related to your spouse's addiction. (Have you done anything inappropriate with our children? Did you ever leave our children alone or unsupervised when you were acting out?)

You can ask about the length of affairs.

We would also encourage you to express how you're feeling about what you've learned as clearly as you can, using "I feel...about...because" statements. It will be very helpful for your spouse to hear from you how his/her behaviors have impacted you and the marriage. And you'll benefit from being honest about what's going on inside of you as you begin the grieving process.

What if I think of other questions later?

Often during a time of disclosure you may be so overwhelmed by what you learn that you are too numb and confused to ask any questions. Later, usually a day or two after the disclosure session, all of those unasked and unanswered questions come to your mind riding a huge wave of anger and anxiety. If and when you experience this tidal wave of fear and doubts and questions, we encourage you to take some time to think about what you're feeling and thinking before you approach your spouse. Many of us have found it helpful to:

Get away by yourself to a place where you can focus and concentrate.

- Invite the Lord to join you in the painful process of fearing and doubting your spouse's integrity and love for you.

- Write down all of your questions.

- Read each question and ask, "Why do I want to know that?"

- Cross out questions that are asking for more details about things you already know.

- Put a star by questions that seem to be valid concerns and need to be addressed.

- Call your counselor and/or group members to ask for feedback on the questions you have marked with a star.

If others agree that your questions are valid, plan a time with your spouse to discuss them. (You may need to set up another counseling appointment if you have a significant number of questions or if you feel your spouse has been dishonest in his/her initial disclosure.)

How can I be sure my spouse has told me everything?

The answer to this question falls somewhere between "You can't," and "You'll know." If your spouse is pursuing God and working diligently on his/her recovery, then over time your spouse will be completely honest with you and eventually disclose everything that you need to know. However, if your spouse is not pursuing recovery, he is probably not going to be honest with you about everything. In that case, God Himself will show you what you need to know.

Do we really believe that? Absolutely. In our own lives and the lives of other spouses we have worked with, God has proved his faithfulness to reveal the truth time and time again. You don't have to be the private detective anymore, but it will take a commitment on your part to leave the investigating and uncovering work to God. That means you must be able to trust God with your spouse. If you're finding yourself consumed with fear and continually looking for evidence of your spouse's sexual behaviors, it might be that you have something in your heart that prevents you from trusting God. On our own journeys we have found it very helpful to look at our own past experiences. Messages we carry from our past greatly influence our ability to trust.

We want to mention here that there may be times that your spouse will need to disclose other pieces of information that they did not share initially. This "multiple disclosure" method happens most often for one of four reasons. First, sexual sin causes a great deal of shame. Whatever behaviors a struggler sees as particularly shameful, they may have a great difficulty sharing – even with a counselor. Second, your spouse may withhold some information at the time of disclosure if they feel that particular behaviors will result in losses they are not ready to face or experience. Third, because some of our spouses have engaged in so many sexual encounters with others, they may actually forget about experiences. Addicts can also have blackouts and not remember what they did during an addictive cycle. Finally, it's very difficult for addicts to witness the pain they've caused others. Sometimes, they just can't bear to see those they love hurt any more and so they omit certain facts during initial disclosure.

The good news is that if your spouse is pursuing healing and recovery, God is actively at work in his/her heart and life. Many times God will remind a struggler of sexual behaviors that they have deliberately withheld. As God works in your spouse's life all of the secrets are being exposed and his/her mind is being renewed and transformed.

The bad news is that we end up grieving all over again when our spouses disclose additional information about their sexual behaviors. If you end up experiencing "multiple disclosures" in your own marriage, remember that your spouse's choices are more about them than about you.

What do I tell my family and close friends?

As you think about disclosing to family and friends, you must determine how much they need to know about your spouse's struggles and behaviors. Most often family members only need to know generalities. Remember, details make the emotional impact of truth much greater. If a family member or friend asks for details, your response should be, "I'm not comfortable answering that question." Be as specific as you can to avoid confusion or unnecessary fears, but limit what you tell family members in order not to expose them to more than they might be able to handle. Keep in mind that you have a support group and probably a counselor to talk to. Most of your family members will have to deal with the bad news without that kind of support. Also, when you talk to family members, remember to use language that they understand and try to express the behavior in a way that shows why it's so hurtful to you.

For example, instead of saying, "Jack is a sex addict," you might say something like, "Jack was unfaithful in our marriage with more than one woman, and I am really struggling with his betrayal." If your spouse is addicted to pornography you could say, "My husband has a problem with pornography that has impacted his ability to relate to me and our children."

Remember that some family members and friends are safer than others. Seek advice and counsel from those in your small group about when and what to share with those you love.

What about our children? What do I tell them?

We firmly believe that disclosing to children in progressive and age-appropriate ways is healing for the child and for the family as a whole. Children are very sensitive to tensions between parents. Often they will blame themselves for marital disagreements and discord. Talking about what they already know validates their feelings and helps them feel connected to you – even if the information you share causes them pain. Preschoolers can understand that Daddy lied to Mommy and hurt her heart very much. Elementary children can grasp the fact that Mommy had a friendship with another person that she should have had only with

Daddy. Teenagers can handle even more information, and adult children should be told the general facts of the situation.

As children grow, we can continue to share more and more of our story with them. We want them to see that God loves us when we behave badly, that there are consequences for our choices, and that God can redeem any situation we give to Him.

One more thing to add—if your spouse is in recovery, the best possible way to disclose to your children is for you and your spouse to sit down together as your spouse shares what he has done and any consequences that will affect the family as a whole. Children need words of security. Don't lie in order to make them feel secure, but do reassure them about the things that won't change during the coming weeks and months. Also, remember to give your children a chance to share how they are feeling and express any fears they may have.

Whose responsibility is it to tell my spouse's parents about the problem?

Often when we find out about our spouse's sexual addiction, the first phone call we make is to our parents. Our spouses, however, may struggle with telling their parents about their problem. Facing the disappointment of parents is a huge hurdle to overcome. In our opinion, however, it is your spouse's responsibility to tell his/her parents – not yours. It's part of the hard work your spouse must do – facing his/her sin and taking responsibility for it. Don't rescue your spouse from that work.

If your spouse is blaming you for the problems in your marriage, it is still not your responsibility to tell your in-laws. You can say, "Your son/daughter is not being completely honest with you. The marriage has been damaged greatly by his/her choices. I'm really hurting right now, but it is his/her responsibility to be honest with you about what is going on." If your spouse's parents really care for you and are interested in knowing the truth, they will confront their child. If they are unhealthy and deceived, then they won't believe anything you tell them anyway.

Should my spouse meet with my parents for a time of reconciliation?

If your parents are aware of the problem, are safe people (i.e. won't meet him at the door with a shotgun), and are willing to talk with your spouse, it can be a very good and Scriptural thing to do. Your family needs to know that your spouse is sorry for what he has done to you and to them. Regardless of how your family members respond, it is a great exercise in obedience and faith for your spouse. However, that plan to meet your parents and apologize should be initiated by your spouse – not you. That's your spouse's stuff. Let God work in your spouse's heart to bring them to that place of maturity and obedience.

What should I do if my spouse doesn't want me to tell anyone about their struggle?

Especially in situations in which the spouse is not working on recovery, this is a very common response. If this is your situation, you will need great discernment and great courage. Tell your spouse that you need a place to talk about how his/her sexual behaviors have impacted you. Assure your spouse that you will use discretion. Then find a counselor, become involved in a confidential support group, and if you have a safe friend or two, share with them as well. Be respectful. Talk to your spouse about the nature of what you are sharing and who you're talking with. But also be firm about getting your heart the help it needs.

You've been greatly impacted by your spouse's sinful choices; it's now your responsibility to make healthy choices and live in such a way that you can heal and grow. You can't heal apart from healthy relationships, so telling safe people is a necessary part of your recovery. You may need a lot of courage to stand by your work if your spouse threatens to leave you, but covering up your spouse's sexual sin in order to save the marriage won't work. You'll be miserable, and the marriage will eventually fall apart. So, be honest with safe people, be truthful with your spouse about who you're sharing with, and trust God to be at work in your spouse's life.

What should I tell acquaintances who are not close friends?

Tell them the truth without sharing any details. Things like, "Yes, we are really struggling right now. I can't really share what's going on, but we are getting help. Please do pray for our marriage." Or you could try being very real. "Thanks for your concern. I really don't know you well enough to share details with you, but I appreciate your prayers for our marriage."

I'm too embarrassed to tell anyone about this. Must I?

Well, that depends on two things: Can you keep from telling others without being dishonest, and can you remain in relationships with others without telling? You have to have people, and you have to have truth. If the truth about your spouse's struggle causes you to isolate yourself from other people, you will never heal. Healing comes in relationship – and not just relationship, but intimate relationship. If you're lying about your situation, you will never heal – and neither will your spouse. It was secrets that got your spouse this far, and it is secrets that will keep your spouse (and you) bound. We can't make you tell safe people about your pain and your struggles, but overcoming your fears and shame will be necessary for you and your spouse to continue on the journey.

What can I expect after disclosure?

After disclosure you will grieve. You'll likely feel numb at first, and then experience anger and sadness and despair. Your spouse may feel better than they have in years, now that all the secrets are out. But you may resent your mate for being so happy when your world has been torn apart. Expect mood swings and tiredness. If you find yourself unable to sleep, eat or function for 14 or more consecutive days, it is time to see a doctor for help.

The most important things you can do after disclosure are to be authentic with your spouse about what you're feeling, and authentic with the friends God has placed in your life. As long as you're talking about what's going on in your heart—the good, the bad and the ugly— you're on the healing journey. Withdrawing and isolating yourself will only limit what God can do in your life to heal your wounds.[14]

---

[14] Adapted from *L.I.F.E. Ministries, A L.I.F.E. Guide for Spouses* by Melissa Haas. Used by permission.

APPENDIX B
Slip vs. Relapse

Slip? Relapse? Does it Really Matter?

So do you call it a slip or a relapse? (Or perhaps a "slip-lapse"?)

Debates continue in Twelve Step rooms as to whether a behavior is a slip or a relapse. There is an easy way of determining how a problem behavior is categorized.

Remember "Dr. Pepper." Or at least remember the acronym DRP. Three words can help you determine whether a behavior is a slip or a relapse.

Duration–How much time did the behavior consume? Granted, this is a subjective differentiation. If a behavior is of a short duration, then it could be considered a slip. But a behavior that is of longer duration would be rightly categorized as a relapse.

Repetition–If a behavior is repeated, regardless of how short the behaviors are, they qualify as a relapse. So a person may have a slip today. But if the behavior is repeated tomorrow, it's not another slip; rather, a relapse started today.

Premeditation–Also, if a behavior is premeditated, even if it is brief and not repeated, then it should also be called a relapse. So if a behavior is anticipated to take place when your spouse is out of town, even if it ends up being of short duration, the behavior should be called a relapse.

So why does it matter? Defining the behavior is important because it determines what type of changes need to be made moving forward. Does the event in question require entering or increasing therapy? Should intensive outpatient services be considered? Or is it time to finally go to an inpatient treatment facility?

And for those who are set on minimizing their behavior by saying, "It was just a slip," a note of caution needs to be heard. Slips and relapses are both serious events. And they require significant changes in recovery to see that the behaviors do not happen again.

What have you learned from a slip or a relapse?

What do you do to make sure they don't happen again?[15]

---

[15] Hope & Freedom Counseling Services. *End Shame: Addiction Recovery Blog.* www.endshame.com, November 25, 2011.

RECOMMENDED BOOKS

Book Categories

Workbooks – focused specifically on recovery for men

Psychological – books for men that take a primarily psychological approach to recovery

Relational – books for men that take a primarily relational and spiritual approach to recovery

Personal – stories from men who have faced sexual brokenness and found healing

Sexuality – books on the topic of sexuality and sexual purity, but not about addiction

Related – books not written about sexual recovery for men, but with significant overlap in content

Workbooks

Freedom Begins Here, *The Personal Toolkit.*

Laaser, Mark, *Faithful & True: Workbook.* Faithful & True Publications, 2015.

Laaser, Mark, The L.I.F.E. Guide for Men. Life Ministries, 2008.

Roberts, Ted, Diane Roberts, Harry Flanagan, *The Seven Pillars of Freedom.* Pure Desire Ministries International, 2015.

Psychological

Carnes, Patrick, *In the Shadows of the Net.* Hazelden, 2007.

Carnes, Patrick, *Out of the Shadows.* Hazelden, 2001.

Laaser, Mark, *Healing the Wounds of Sexual Addiction.* Zondervan, 2004.

Perkins, Bill, *When Good Men are Tempted.* Zondervan, 2007.

Strutters, William M., *Wired for Intimacy.* IVP Books, 2010.

Weiss, Doug, *Clean.* Thomas Nelson, 2013.

Weiss, Doug, *Sex, Men and God.* Siloam, 2002.

Weiss, Doug, *The Final Freedom.* Discovery Press, 1998.

Wilson, Earl, *Steering Clear.* IVP Books, 2002

Relational

Anderson, Neil T., *Winning the Battle Within.* Harvest House Publishers, 2008.

Bodishbaugh, Signa and Conlee, *Illusions of Intimacy.* Sovereign World, 2004.

Dallas, Joe, *The Game Plan.* Thomas Nelson, 2005.

Daugherty, Jonathan, *Grace-Based Recovery.* Lulu.com, 2013.

Gallagher, Steve, *At the Altar of Sexual Idolatry*. Pure Life Ministries, 2000.

Gross, Craig, *Open*. Thomas Nelson, 2013.

Laaser, Mark, *Becoming a Man of Valor*. Beacon Hill Press, 2011.

Laaser, Mark, *Taking Every Thought Captive*. Beacon Hill Press, 2011.

Roberts, Ted, *Pure Desire*. Bethany House Publishers, 2008.

Schaumburg, Harry, *False Intimacy*. NavPress, 1997.

Schaumburg, Harry, *Undefined*. Moody Publishers, 2009.

Personal Stories

Crosse, Clay, Renee Crosse, Mark Tabb, *I Surrender All*. NavPress, 2005.

Daugherty, Jonathan, *Secrets*. Tate Publishing, 2009.

Leahy, Michael, *Porn Nation*. Northfields Publishing, 2008.

Zailer, David, *When Lost Men Come Home*. Operation Integrity, 2012.

Sexuality

Alcorn, Randy, *The Purity Principle*. Multnomah, 2003.

Gross, Craig, Steven Luff, *Pure Eyes*. Baker Books, 2010.

Harris, Joshua, *Sex is Not the Problem (Lust is)*. Multnomah, 2005.

Parrott, Les, *Crazy Good Sex*. Zondervan, 2011.

Related Books

Allender, Dan, *The Wounded Heart*. NavPress, 2008.

Eldridge, John, *Wild at Heart*. Thomas Nelson, 2001.

Fort, John W., *The Other Side of Black Rock*. CreateSpace Independent Publishing, 2013.

Laaser, Mark, *7 Principles of Highly Accountable Men*. Beacon Hill Press, 2011.

Lynch, John, Bruce McNicol, Bill Thrall, *Bo's Cafe*. Windblown Media, 2009.

Lynch, John, Bruce McNicol, Bill Thrall, *The Cure*. NavPress, 2011.

May, Gerald, *Addiction & Grace*. Haperone, 2006.

McGee, Robert, *The Search for Significance*. Thomas Nelson, 2003.

VanVonderen, Jeff, *Tired of Trying to Measure Up*. Bethany House Publishers, 2008.

GLOSSARY

GLOSSARY

The following definitions should be considered within the context of the sexual healing journey.

Accountability

An agreement between two or more individuals regarding a predetermined set of expectations surrounding one's choices to live pure.

Accountability Line

A list of one's most destructive behaviors to be stopped, along with some needs these attempt to meet. It further includes positive behaviors to be substituted for negative ones. This is a dynamic document to be changed as often as needed. It should be shared with one's support group, wife and trusted others. (Formerly referred to as a *Sobriety line*.)

Acting Out

An unhealthy sexual action that expresses what one is internally experiencing and desiring to do (e.g. look at pornography, masturbate or actually have sexual contact with another person).

Authenticity

Realness; genuineness; when what is true on the inside of someone corresponds with what is experienced by others in relationship with them.

Behaviorism

A focus on correcting unhealthy or abnormal behavior rather than addressing the causes of such behavior.

Betrayal

The breaking or violation of a trust or confidence that produces moral and psychological (emotional) conflict within a relationship.

Compulsive

Resulting from or relating to an irresistible urge, especially one that is against ones' conscious wishes.

Cruising

The instinctive search for some kind of sexual stimulation (e.g. channel surfing, cruising the web, deciding to go for a drive past locations to act out). These are often known as rituals—behavior that precedes unhealthy sexual behavior.

Destination Thinking

Believing that a long-term problem can have a short-term resolution, bypassing all of the time-consuming and ongoing steps required for lasting change and healing.

Disclosure

The process in which a person struggling with sexual addiction tells others about his/her sexual behaviors.

Emotional Pain

A profoundly unpleasant feeling of a non-physical origin (e.g. loneliness, betrayal, failure, depression, anger).

Fantasy

Imagining things that are impossible or improbable for the purpose of escaping a painful or overwhelming reality.

Father Wound

The emotional pain experienced by a child that results when the child's father fails to meet needs that would normally be met in a healthy relationship. This leaves the child having to find substitute ways to meet those needs.

FMO

Abbreviation for Pure Life Alliance's For Men Only ministry consisting of weekly men's support groups that exist to hold men accountable to walking in purity.

Guilt

The feeling and awareness of having done wrong. Can be a positive emotion if it turns one back to God.

Hot-wired Sexuality

Childhood sexualization that occurs prior to puberty. This can result in shame, isolation and a fear of being known.

Intimacy

Mental, emotional and physical closeness requiring clear boundaries between two people which allow them to be truly seen for who they are. This allows for disclosure of self without expectations.

Journey Thinking

A mindset allowing for time to heal and process new truths. Focuses on the experience and process of change and growth as a goal within itself, as opposed to destination thinking.

Lust

To covet, strongly desire, or set your heart on something, generally in the negative sense. To allow oneself to desire what is not rightfully yours.

Mentor

A man with more experience on his recovery journey who meets with, listens to, and guides a less experienced man.

Mentor Manual

A Pure Life Alliance For Men Only three-module training designed to provide a man information appropriate to the place he is at on his purity journey.

Purity

Freedom from sexual immorality (see *Sobriety*).

Recovery

The journey from shame and secrecy, characterized by compulsive behaviors, toward peace and authenticity, characterized by honesty and purity.

Restoration

The action of returning a relationship to a former condition.

Ritual

The act of beginning to physically fulfill a sexual fantasy (e.g. channel surfing, cruising the web, deciding to go for a drive past locations to act out).

Sex Addiction

Obsession or preoccupation with sexual themes. Includes compulsive behavior despite negative consequences.

Shame (Toxic)

A longterm, destructive emotion that leads a person to believe they are worthless, less than or bad. An internal self-assessment of who one is—as a person—as opposed to what one does.

Shame Cycle

A destructive cycle driven by shame. The cycle includes acting out, temporary numbness, emotional pain, shame and cruising.

Sobriety

The standard of sexual behavior you require of yourself. (See *Purity*).

Sobriety Line

See *Accountability Line*

Substitutions

Positive actions that can replace acting out.

Support Group

A group of individuals who encourage each other over the common problem of sexually compulsive behavior. See For Men Only.

Survival Guide

See *Mentor Manual.*

Temporary Numbness

Short-term relief of the power of negative feelings.

Trigger

Feelings or events that lead to an immediate attempt to escape unwanted feelings. An event or circumstance that leads to a particular sexual thought, feeling, behavior or action.

ACKNOWLEDGMENTS

This book has passed through a long and harrowing journey, not unlike the path a sex addict must follow. Years in the making, it encompasses the contributions of many friends, some of whom are still in ministry with Pure Life Alliance.

John Fort—While no longer on staff at PLA, John's insights and contributions to this volume are immeasurable. His desire and vision for a multi-module manual (say that three times fast!) helped sharpen the effectiveness of this first module. Thank you, John, for bringing your experience and knowledge to bear on this first installment.

Vince Corbin—Vince joined the initial team of three to kick off this effort. He has been on the journey the longest of all three and is well-versed in both the theory of recovery and the practical experience in recovery. Through many meetings, Vince's "roll up the sleeves" approach to tweaking a writing outline made this final product what it is today. His influence in creating the new shame cycle model (see p.43) will impact many. Vince, your fingerprints are all over this effort...thank you.

Blake Williams—As PLA's Executive Director, Blake was blessed with both passion and clarity that often slowed the writing process to a crawl. But this has also ensured a study well aligned with the "First Steps" of a new man's purity journey. Blake, thanks for investing your heart in the lives of so many through this book.

The FMO Mentor Team—Phil Brothers and David Burleson are two men every one of you should know. Each of them spent weekly planning meetings adjusting the final version of this module. Furthermore, they each have played a vital role in crafting the whole mentor manual project in scope, depth and divisions. David's investment in writing the masturbation chapter brought a fresh perspective to an awkward—yet needed—lesson. Phil's editing input as well as his almost-single-handedly defining terms in the Glossary proved his own maturity on the journey. Gentlemen, it is an honor doing ministry with you.

Melissa Williams—One of the topics covered in FMO's companion ministry Hidden Hurt is that of sexual intimacy. The source material for the Restoring Intimacy lesson was shamelessly stolen (with her permission, of course) from Melissa's teaching notes. Without Melissa's valuable input from a woman's perspective, this lesson would be much less than it is. Melissa, thank you for your passion to exhort men and women to live well, even in the bedroom.

CJ Chang—Editor extraordinaire. CJ's ability to rework cumbersome sentences has been a gift beyond compare. Bringing an end to run-on sentences, repositioning dangling modifiers and removing unnecessary punctuation was her challenge—and she did it with aplomb. CJ, thank you for investing your skills on this humble project. It is remarkably better because of your efforts.

Those who paved the way for this mentor manual—Pure Life Alliance has been blessed to be using a mentor manual called *Survival Guide: A Mentored Guide to Begin Your Journey Toward Purity*. Since 2006, we have matched mentors with new men using this well-written tool. The men who invested in that effort deserve to be mentioned here—their efforts are deeply appreciated: John Canlas, Mitch Frey, John Fort, Glenn Molloy, Mike Umbriaco, William Waterman and Blake Williams.

Dennis Henderson—During a Pastor Lunch at Sunset Presbyterian in 2003, Dr. Henderson first planted the idea of mentoring new men just beginning their journey. Were it not for his simply stated and well-argued perspective on that day, it is unlikely you would be holding this manual right now. And so it is most appropriate that we asked him to write the Foreword for this manual. Dennis, thank you for investing so much in so many.

Made in the USA
San Bernardino, CA
27 April 2017